MATHS PLUS
FROM HEINEMANN

Games and Puzzles
for the Key Objectives

2

Peter Clarke

Heinemann

Halley Court, Jordan Hill, Oxford, OX2 8EJ
a division of Reed Educational and Professional Publishing Ltd
www.heinemann.co.uk

Heinemann is a registered trademark of Reed Educational and Professional Publishing Ltd

ISBN   0 435 03251 8

04   03
10 9 8 7 6 5 4

Typeset by D.P. Press Ltd, Sevenoaks
Illustrated by Juliette Nicholson and Chris Ryley
Printed and bound in Great Britain by Ashford Colour Press, Gosport, Hants

Contents

Introduction

Games and Puzzles for the Key Objectives is a series of seven books from Reception to Year 6. It provides a range of quick and easy games and puzzles designed to practise and consolidate the key objectives from the National Numeracy Strategy (NNS) *Framework*. The mathematical activities included in this book are suitable for 6- to 7-year-olds, although individual teachers or schools may also decide to use them with other year groups.

Why include games and puzzles in the maths curriculum?

Games and puzzles enhance the mathematics curriculum in many ways. They provide:
- an opportunity for children to communicate with each other and develop new mathematical language
- a non-threatening and enjoyable way for children to consolidate their understanding of mathematical skills and concepts
- a chance for children to use and apply mathematical skills and concepts which have been mastered in more formal learning contexts
- an informal assessment tool to help you determine whether children are able to use and apply mathematical skills in a real-life recreational setting
- an opportunity for children to play co-operatively together.

Curriculum information

All the activities are organized under the specific key objective as identified in the NNS *Framework*; they therefore have direct links to the *National Curriculum Programmes of Study for Key Stage 1*. They are suitable for children working at Levels A–B in *Mathematics 5–14* (for a more detailed curriculum coverage for Scotland see page viii).

The activities

For each of the key objectives there is a range of different activities. These include:
- *Games* – purpose-driven games which involve pair or group work and create an engaging forum for discussion and feedback between children and teachers.
- *Puzzles* – tasks generally requiring children to work alone, applying their mathematical knowledge, skills and reasoning abilities to solve problems.

Many of the games also include ideas for variations. Where these extend the activity, they are marked ↑ and where they simplify the activity, they are marked ↓ .

How to use this book

The activities are flexible enough to be used in a variety of ways. For example, activities might be chosen:
- for the whole class during the oral work and mental calculation session
- for individuals, pairs or groups of children during the practice and consolidation session
- for individual children or groups of children who finish early and need additional stimulus at the end of the practice and consolidation session
- for the whole class during the plenary session
- for individual children to do at home.

While all the activities suggest the number of children involved, many can easily be adapted to cater for any number of children, including the whole class.

Working with other adults

Many of the activities contained in this book can be used with groups of children working on the same activity either individually, in pairs or as a group. If other adults are available to support the children, they should be thoroughly briefed about the activity and their particular role in it. They should be aware of not only what the children are to do but also what children are to learn. If they are sensitive to the particular needs of the children, adults can:
- help develop new mathematical skills and concepts and reinforce or extend those already acquired
- help develop new mathematical language
- encourage appropriate methods of recording
- assess understanding of particular mathematical concepts and vocabulary
- give feedback on progress to both the children and the teacher.

Assessment

All the activities in this book practise and consolidate children's understanding of the key objectives for Year 2. These key objectives, as identified by the NNS, are the key concepts and skills children are required to achieve by the end of Year 2. They should therefore be given priority when planning work and assessing children's progress. By assessing the children (either formally or informally) whilst they are undertaking these activities, useful insights may be gained into the misconceptions of individuals or groups of children. This will help to identify weaknesses, where further teaching is required, and strengths, where challenging opportunities are appropriate.

Introducing maths games to the children

The following points will help support children's efforts to play the maths games on their own.

- Ensure that the children are familiar and secure with the mathematical skills and concepts being practised in the game.
- If all the children in the class will be playing the game during a short period of time (say a week or two), introduce it during a whole-class session.
- Play the game, with you playing against the class. It may be useful to make a copy of the game board onto an overhead transparency or a large sheet of paper. Ensure that you complete the game with the children, making clear all the rules and how the game is won.

Materials

This series limits materials to a small range of simple, readily available resources. The main resources are:

- 0–10/0–20 number tracks
- 0–9/0–10 number cards
- counters
- various dice (dotted and numbered)
- interlocking cubes

Where an activity requires dice, cards or counters, this is indicated on the Classroom organization chart (pages vi–vii).

Constructing the maths games

For the activities which use game boards, you will need the following materials:

- copies of the game boards and instructions
- copies of game cards (if applicable)
- thick card
- glue
- scissors
- medium-sized envelopes
- crayons or markers
- large plastic sleeves

1. Photocopy the game board onto one side of thick card and the instructions onto the other side. (If this is not possible, photocopy onto paper and stick onto card.) If the game also requires game cards, photocopy these onto thick card, cut out and place in an envelope.
2. Use crayons or markers to decorate the game board and game cards.
3. Clearly label the game board and instructions with the game's name.
4. Place the game board and instructions, game cards (if applicable) and any other required resources (counters, dice and so on) into a large plastic sleeve. You may also want to label the front of the plastic sleeve.
5. Place the game in a maths games box and store centrally.

General tips for use

- Make multiple copies of games if you want more than one group of children to be able to play at the same time.
- Allow some time in your weekly planning for games and puzzles.
- Adjust the rules, alter the numbers, vary the materials, simplify the language or change the number of players to suit children's needs.
- Invite children who have played the game to teach their peers what to do.
- Take time to play the games with individual children. This helps them to become more confident with the mathematics and better at the game, as well as helping you to assess their understanding.
- Plan a 'Games morning/evening'. Invite parents to play the games with the children to better appreciate the value of mathematical games.
- Provide simple mathematical puzzles as homework tasks.
- Send the plastic sleeves containing the games home overnight so that children can play with adults at home.

Classroom organization chart

Key objective	Title	Players	Resources			Page
			dice	cards	counters	
Describe and extend simple number sequences: count on or back in ones or tens starting from any 2-digit number.	1.1 Go on, go back	2	1–6		✓	1
	1.2 Stop the count!	2		1–100		2
	1.3 1 or 10 more or less	1				2
	1.4 Make a set	class		1–100		3
	1.5 Stepping stones	class		1–100		3
	1.6 How many steps?	1				3
Describe and extend simple number sequences: recognize odd and even numbers.	2.1 Odd bubbles	2			✓	4
	2.2 Move on odd or even	2	1–6		✓	5
	2.3 Odds and evens total	2	0–9		✓	6
	2.4 Collecting odd or even	2	0–9		✓	6
	2.5 Evens takeaway	2–4	1–6		✓	6
	2.6 Land on even	2–4	1–6		✓	7
	2.7 Odd or even?	class				7
	2.8 Odd and even bingo	class				7
Read and write whole numbers to at least 100.	3.1 Cover the number names	2	0–9		✓	8
	3.2 What's the number?	2		0–9		9
	3.3 Write the number name	2–4		0–100		9
	3.4 Show me the number	class		0–9		9
Know what each digit in a 2-digit number represents, including 0 as a place holder.	4.1 100 square place value	2		playing 0–9		10
	4.2 Make a 2-digit number	2–4			✓	11
	4.3 I've got the tens and units	up to 4 or class			✓	12
	4.4 Place value loop	class				14
Order whole numbers to at least 100.	5.1 Correct order number cards	2		0–50		16
	5.2 Number tiles	2–4				17
	5.3 100 square pictures	1				19
	5.4 100 square puzzles	1				20
	5.5 Order the children	group/class				20
Understand that subtraction is the inverse of addition; state the subtraction corresponding to a given addition and vice versa.	6.1 Match the facts	2				21
	6.2 Give me the inverse	2		1–20		21
	6.3 To the board	class				21
Know by heart all addition and subtraction facts for each number to at least 10.	7.1 Cover the stars	2	1–6		✓	22
	7.2 Add or subtract balloons	2	1–6		✓	23
	7.3 Make a line	2	1–6		✓	24
	7.4 Number line difference	2	0–9		✓	25
	7.5 In a minute	2–4	0–9			25
	7.6 Ping-pong facts	2				25
	7.7 Addition and subtraction bingo	group/class		0–10	✓	26
	7.8 Say it and you're out	class				28
	7.9 Addition lottery	class				28
	7.10 Coin combinations	1				28
	7.11 Magic number puzzles	1				29
Use knowledge that addition can be done in any order to do mental calculations more efficiently.	8.1 Lu-Lu: a variation on a Polynesian adding game	2–4			✓	30
	8.2 Same calculation?	2				30
	8.3 Make the number	1				30
	8.4 Magic squares	1				31
	8.5 Cross additions	1				31
Understand the operation of multiplication as repeated addition or as describing an array.	9.1 Add the number thrown	2	1–6		✓	32
	9.2 Draw an array	2		2–10		33
	9.3 Write the calculation	2				33
	9.4 The array game	2			✓	33

Classroom organization chart *cont.*

Key objective	Title	Players	dice	cards	counters	Page
Know and use halving as the inverse of doubling.	10.1 Double and half	2				34
	10.2 Doubling game	2–4	1–6		✓	35
	10.3 Halving game	2–4	1–6		✓	36
	10.4 Forward, double, back	2–4	1–6		✓	37
	10.5 Double up	class	1–6			37
	10.6 Twice as much	1				37
Know by heart multiplication facts for the 2 and 10 multiplication tables.	11.1 Multiplication tic-tac-toe	2	0–9		✓	38
	11.2 First to cover	2	0–9		✓	39
	11.3 Stack them up	2	0–9		✓	39
	11.4 Know the facts	2		0–9	✓	41
	11.5 Whole class multiplication	class		0–9		41
	11.6 Three in a row	2–4		1–100		41
Choose and use appropriate operations and efficient calculation strategies to solve problems, explaining how the problem was solved.	12.1 Loop problems	class				42
	12.2 Match the cards	2				44
	12.3 Problem-solving game	2	1–6		✓	45
Estimate, measure and compare lengths, masses and capacities, using standard units; suggest suitable units and equipment for such measurements. Read a simple scale to the nearest labelled division, including using a ruler to draw and measure lines to the nearest centimetre.	Length					
	13.1 Going home	2	1–6			46
	13.2 Which is longer?	2			✓	47
	13.3 Estimate and measure my length	2–4			✓	48
	13.4 I spy	3–4 or class			✓	48
	13.5 Draw me a line	class				48
	Mass					
	13.6 More, less and exactly a kilogram	1				49
	13.7 Estimate and measure the weight	2–4			✓	49
	Capacity					
	13.8 How many?	class				49
Use the mathematical names for common 2D and 3D shapes; sort shapes and describe some of their features.	14.1 Shapes and names	2				50
	14.2 Name the shapes	3–4				52
	14.3 How many shapes?	1				52
	14.4 Matchsticks	1				52
	14.5 Sort the shapes	2				53
	14.6 Describe the shapes	group				53
	14.7 Label the shapes	2–4				53
Use mathematical vocabulary to describe position, direction and movement.	15.1 Collect the counters	2	1–6		✓	54
	15.2 Class positions	2–4	1–6		✓	55
	15.3 Treasure maps	2				56
	15.4 Find the bear	group/class				56
	15.5 Simon says turn	group/class				56

Curriculum matches

Scotland: Match to *Mathematics 5–14*

The activities in this book are appropriate for children working at Levels A–B.

Attainment targets	Strands	Pages
Information handling	Collect	
	Organize	
	Display	
	Interpret	
Number, money and measurement	Range and type of numbers	8–20
	Money	
	Add and subtract	21–31, 42–5
	Multiply and divide	32–45
	Round numbers	
	Fractions, percentages and ratio	
	Patterns and sequences	1–7
	Functions and equations	
	Measure and estimate	46–9
	Time	
Shape, position and movement	Range of shapes	50–53
	Position and movement	54–6
	Symmetry	
	Angle	

Northern Ireland: Match to *Lines of development*

The activities in this book are suitable for children working at Levels 2–3.

Key objective	Pages	Reference to *Lines of development*
Describe and extend simple number sequences: count on or back in ones or tens starting from any 2-digit number.	1–3	R2.4
Describe and extend simple number sequences: recognize odd and even numbers.	4–7	R2.5, R1.4
Read and write whole numbers to at least 100.	8–9	N2.9
Know what each digit in a 2-digit number represents, including 0 as a place holder.	10–15	N2.11
Order whole numbers to at least 100.	16–20	N2.11
Understand that subtraction is the inverse of addition; state the subtraction corresponding to a given addition and vice versa.	21	N2.2
Know by heart all addition and subtraction facts for each number to at least 10.	22–9	N1.22
Use knowledge that addition can be done in any order to do mental calculations more efficiently.	30–31	
Understand the operation of multiplication as repeated addition or as describing an array.	32–3	N2.27
Know and use halving as the inverse of doubling.	34–7	
Know by heart multiplication facts for the 2 and 10 multiplication tables.	38–41	
Choose and use appropriate operations and efficient calculation strategies to solve problems, explaining how the problem was solved.	42–5	
Estimate, measure and compare lengths, masses and capacities, using standard units; suggest suitable units and equipment for such measurements. Read a simple scale to the nearest labelled division, including using a ruler to draw and measure lines to the nearest centimetre.	46–9	all M3 statements
Use the mathematical names for common 2D and 3D shapes; sort shapes and describe some of their features.	50–53	S3.2, S3.3
Use mathematical vocabulary to describe position, direction and movement.	54–6	Sp3.4

Wales: Match to *Key Stage 1 Programme of study*

The activities in this book are appropriate for children working at Levels 2–3. Opportunities for Using and Applying are provided throughout.

Key objective	Pages	Number				Shape, space and measure		
		1. Understanding number and place value	2. Understanding number relationships and methods of calculation	3. Solving numerical problems	4. Classifying, representing and interpreting data	1. Understanding and using patterns and properties of shape	2. Understanding and using properties of position and movement	3. Understanding and using measures
Describe and extend simple number sequences: count on or back in ones or tens starting from any 2-digit number.	1–3		●					
Descrbe and extend simple number sequences: recognize odd and even numbers.	4–7	●	●					
Read and write whole numbers to at least 100.	8–9	●						
Know what each digit in a 2-digit number represents, including 0 as a place holder.	10–15	●						
Order whole numbers to at least 100.	16–20	●						
Understand that subtraction is the inverse of addition; state the subtraction corresponding to a given addition and vice versa.	21		●	●				
Know by heart all addition and subtraction facts for each number to at least 10.	22–9		●					
Use knowledge that addition can be done in any order to do mental calculations more efficiently.	30–31		●					
Understand the operation of multiplication as repeated addition or as describing an array.	32–3			●				
Know and use halving as the inverse of doubling.	34–7		●					
Know by heart multiplication facts for the 2 and 10 multiplication tables.	38–41		●					
Choose and use appropriate operations and efficient calculation strategies to solve problems, explaining how the problem was solved.	42–5			●				
Estimate, measure and compare lengths, masses and capacities, using standard units; suggest suitable units and equipment for such measurements. Read a simple scale to the nearest labelled division, including using a ruler to draw and measure lines to the nearest centimetre.	46–9							●
Use the mathematical names for common 2D and 3D shapes; sort shapes and describe some of their features.	50–53					●		
Use mathematical vocabulary to describe position, direction and movement.	54–6						●	

1.1 ▶ Go on, go back

 2

What you need

- game board
- 1–6 number die
- different coloured counter per child

What to do

- Children place their counter on 1. They take turns to roll the die and move their counter that number of spaces.

If they land on a square marked ◯ they move on one space.

If they land on a square marked ✦ they move back one space.

If they land on a square marked ▢ they move on ten spaces.

If they land on a square marked ☁ they move back ten spaces.

- The winner is the first child to reach 100.

1	2	3	4	5	6	7	8	9	10
11	12	13	14	15	16	17	18	19	20
21	22	23	24	25	26	27	28	29	30
31	32	33	34	35	36	37	38	39	40
41	42	43	44	45	46	47	48	49	50
51	52	53	54	55	56	57	58	59	60
61	62	63	64	65	66	67	68	69	70
71	72	73	74	75	76	77	78	79	80
81	82	83	84	85	86	87	88	89	90
91	92	93	94	95	96	97	98	99	100

1.2 ▷ Stop the count!

 2

What you need

- set of 1–100 number cards

What to do

- Shuffle the number cards and give each child a pile of ten which they should hold facing them.
- Starting from one, both children count on in unison in ones. When they reach a number that either of them is holding, that child says *Stop* and puts down their card. They then continue to count on from that number, stopping every time they reach a number on one of their cards.
- The winner is the first child to put down all their cards.

Variations

↑ Start at 100 and count back.

↑ Tell the children to decide whether to count on or back in ones.

- Children choose a starting number by turning over one of the remaining number cards, then count on or back in ones or tens until they reach one of their cards and put this one down. When they reach a card, or if neither child has a number in that sequence, they begin again with a different starting number.

1.3 ▷ 1 or 10 more or less

 1

What you need

- paper and pencil

What to do

- Draw the following on the board.
- Ask the children to copy and complete the missing 100 square numbers.

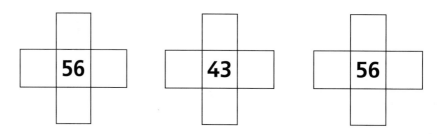

Variations

- Change the numbers.
- Write a number in one of the other squares.

.4 Make a set

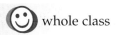 whole class

What you need

- sets of five consecutive number cards (e.g. 42, 43, 44, 45, 46; 74, 75, 76, 77, 78), enough for one card per child

What to do

- Distribute the cards amongst the children at random. Ask them to find the other children in their set and stand in numerical order.
- Choose one set and ask the first and last child in that set to show their cards. *What are the missing numbers?* Ask another set to name the three middle numbers. That set then shows their first and last numbers for the next set to fill in the missing numbers.
- Continue until all the sets have been identified.

.5 Stepping stones

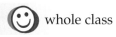 whole class

What you need

- set of 1–100 number cards
- five carpet tiles or A4 pieces of paper

What to do

- Put the carpet tiles or paper on the floor in a row.
- Explain to the children that these are stepping stones across a river which has crocodiles in it. They can only get across by saying the correct number for each stepping stone.
- Place a number card on the first stone and ask a child to count on four in ones from that number. For example, if you put 37 on the first stone, the child counts *37, 38, 39, 40, 41* to cross the river safely. If they make a mistake, they fall in the river. You can choose whether they have another life or get eaten by a crocodile!
- Use a different starting number for each child.

Variations

↑ Count back in ones.
↑ Count on or back in tens.
↑↓ Vary the level of difficulty according to the child's ability, for example crossing or not crossing a tens boundary.

.6 How many steps?

 1

What you need

- no resources needed

What to do

- Write on the board the beginning of a number sequence formed by counting on in steps of one or ten, for example 57, 67, 77, 87, 97 (counting on in tens) or 33, 34, 44, 45, 55, 56 (counting on in alternate ones and tens).
- Give the children a target number for each sequence, perhaps 217 for the first example above and 99 for the second. Can they work out the pattern and tell you how many steps it takes to get from the last number you have given them to the target number?

Variations

- To check the answer, ask one child to stand in front of the class and take appropriate number of steps. The others can count and see if they agree.
↑ Children can play as a pair making up patterns for each other.

2.1 ▷ Odd bubbles

 2

What you need

- game board
- 40 counters

What to do

- Children place a counter on each of the 40 bubbles on the game board.
- They then take turns to remove either one, two or three counters from the game board, as they choose.
- When all the counters have been removed, the child with an odd number of counters is the winner.

Variation

The winner is the child with an even number of counters.

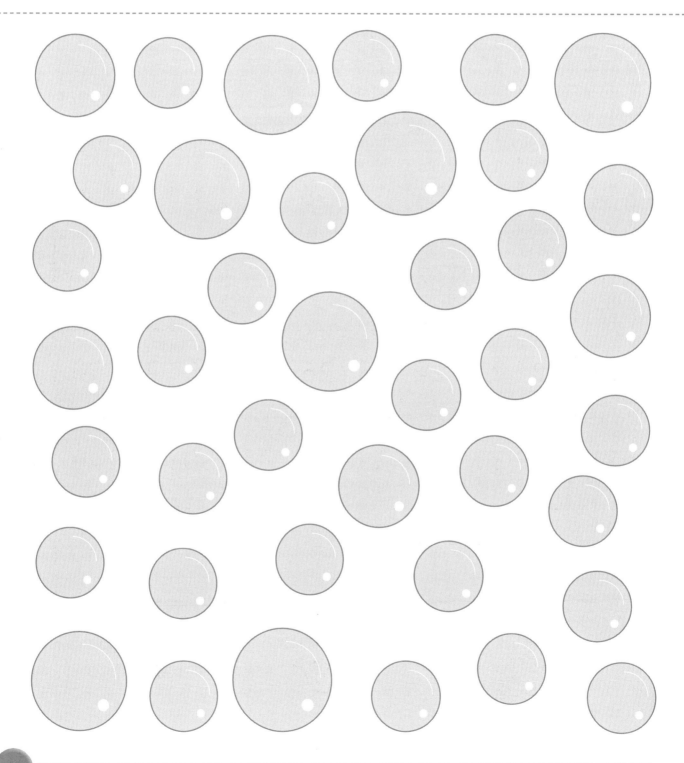

.2   Move on odd or even

 2

What you need

- game board
- two 1–6 number dice
- different coloured counter per child

What to do

- Children decide who is going to move on even numbers (Child A) and who is going to move on odd numbers (Child B).
- Both children place their counter on 1.
- Each child rolls a die and the numbers are added together. If the total is even, Child A moves their counter that number of spaces. If the total is odd, Child B moves their counter that number of spaces.
- The winner is the first child to reach or pass 50.

Variations

↑ Use two 0–9 dice.

↓ Only use one die. Children move the number shown on the die.

1	2	3	4	5	6	7	8	9	10
11	12	13	14	15	16	17	18	19	20
21	22	23	24	25	26	27	28	29	30
31	32	33	34	35	36	37	38	39	40
41	42	43	44	45	46	47	48	49	50

2.3 ▷ Odds and evens total 2

What you need

- two 0–9 dice
- 21 counters

What to do

- Children decide who is going to collect even numbers and who is going to collect odd numbers.
- Each child rolls a die. Both children find the total of the two dice and decide whether the answer is odd or even. If the total is odd, the child collecting odd numbers takes a counter. If the total is even, the child collecting even numbers takes a counter.
- The winner is the child with the most counters after all the counters have been collected.

Variations

↓ Use two 1–6 number dice.

↑ Children write down their numbers rather than taking counters. After ten rolls, they add up their totals. The winner is the child with the larger total.

2.4 ▷ Collecting odd or even 2

What you need

- two 0–9 dice
- 21 counters

What to do

- Children decide who is going to collect even numbers and who is going to collect odd numbers.
- They take turns to roll both dice and use the numbers shown to make two 2-digit numbers. For example, if a child rolls 3 and 8, the two 2-digit numbers are 38 and 83.
- If an odd and an even number are made, each child takes a counter. If two odd (or two even) numbers are made, the child who is collecting odd (or even) numbers takes two counters.
- The game continues until all the counters have been used. The winner is the child with more counters.

2.5 ▷ Evens takeaway 2–4

What you need

- two 1–6 number dice
- 0–30 number line per child
- different coloured counter per child

What to do

- All the children start with their counter on 30 on their number line. They take turns to roll the two dice. If the total of a child's numbers is even, they count back along the number line; if it is odd, they do not move. For example, if a child rolled a 5 and a 1 the total would be 6, so they would count back from 30 to 24. Encourage the children to count back in twos.
- The winner is the first child to reach or pass 0 with their counter.

Variations

↓ Children can start at 0 and add on the even totals they roll, up to 30.

- Children can add or take away odd totals, staying where they are if they roll an even total.

2.6 ⟩ Land on even

 2–4

What you need

- game board (page 6)
- 1–6 number die
- pile of counters

What to do

- Each child chooses a different coloured counter to place on 1.
- Children take turns to roll the die and move their counter that number of spaces.
- If the counter lands on an even number, the child takes a counter from the pile.
- The game continues like this until all the children reach or pass 50 or until there are no more counters left.
- The winner is the child with most counters.

Variation

Play 'Land on odd'. If the counter lands on an odd number, the child takes a counter.

2.7 ⟩ Odd or even?

 whole class

What you need

- one odd and one even card per child, e.g.

What to do

- Call out numbers between 0 and 100.
- Children have to decide whether the number is odd or even and hold up the appropriate card. If they are wrong, they lose a life and stand up. If they lose another life, they stand on one leg. If they lose three lives, they are out.
- The winner is the last child or children left in.

Variation

Rather than calling out numbers, hold up a card from a set of 0–100 number cards.

2.8 ⟩ Odd and even bingo

 whole class

What you need

- paper and pencil per child

What to do

- Children write down any ten numbers from 0 to 100.
- Call out the words *Odd* and *Even* several times in a random order. (Be sure to keep a record for checking purposes.)
- Children cross off one number only that is odd or even as called.
- The winner is the first child to cross out all of their numbers.

3.1 ▷ Cover the number names

 2

What you need

- game board
- two 0–9 dice
- 40 counters (20 of one colour, 20 of another)

What to do

- Children take turns to roll both dice. They use the dice values to make a 2-digit number. For example, if 3 and 7 were rolled, the 2-digit number would be 37 or 73.
- If the number is on the game board, the child covers up the number name using one of their counters. If the number is not on the game board, they miss a turn.
- If all the numbers get covered with counters, the winner is the child with more counters on the board. If all the numbers do not get covered, it may be necessary to set a time limit to determine the end of the game.

Variations

- The first child to make a row of three counters vertically, horizontally or diagonally is the winner.
- Provide each child with a game board. Children use a pack of playing cards with the tens and picture cards removed. They take turns to turn over two cards and try to arrange them to make one of the 2-digit numbers on the board.

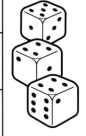

twenty-one	fifty-one	seventy-four
seventy-seven	twelve	thirty-two
fifty	forty-six	ninety-one
seventy-two	eighty-eight	twenty
thirty-seven	twenty-five	sixty-nine
sixteen	ninety-three	forty-eight
eighty-two	fifty-three	eighty-three
forty-four	seventy-five	twenty-three
ninety	fifty-five	thirteen
ninety-six	thirty-nine	sixty-six

3.2   What's the number? 2

What you need

- two sets of 0–9 number cards

What to do

- Children take turns to write a 2-digit number (in figures) with their finger on the table.
- The other child has to show the number using the number cards. If they are correct, they take the number cards which correspond to the two digits of the number. Each digit can, therefore, only be used twice.
- The winner is the child with more number cards when they have all been taken.

Variations

- Children write the number in the air; on their partner's hand; on their partner's back.
- Children write the number in words.
- Use the number names cut out from the game board on page 8.

3.3   Write the number name 2–4

What you need

- set of 0–100 number cards
- paper and pencil per child

What to do

- The number cards are shuffled and placed face down in a pile in the middle of the table.
- Children take turns to pick up a card, for example 82, and write down the number in figures and words, i.e. 82, eighty-two. The child's score for that round is the number of letters in the word, in this case 9.
- The winner is the child with the highest total score.

3.4   Show me the number 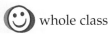 whole class

What you need

- set of 0–9 number cards per child

What to do

- Write a 2-digit number in words on the board or OHP, for example, twenty-six.
- The first child to show the number correctly using their number cards comes to the front and writes another 2-digit number on the board for the rest of the class to show.

Variation

Children use place value cards.

4.1 ▷ 100 square place value

 2

What you need

- record sheet
- pack of playing cards with the tens and picture cards removed
- different coloured pencil per child

What to do

- Explain to the children that aces count as 1.
- Children place the red cards in one pile to represent the tens and the black cards in another pile to represent the units.
- Children take turns to choose a card from each pile, read the 2-digit number and write it in the correct space on the record sheet. If a number is already on the grid, the child notes it at the side.
- If the children run out of cards, shuffle the packs and place the cards back in two piles.
- Children score ten points for each row or column they complete (by writing the final missing number). When the grid is completed, they total their points and deduct two for each number they have noted at the side. The winner is the child with the higher total.

Variation

Place all the cards in one pile. Children choose the top two cards, for example 4 and 9, make a 2-digit number and write it on the grid, i.e. 49 or 94. The game continues as above.

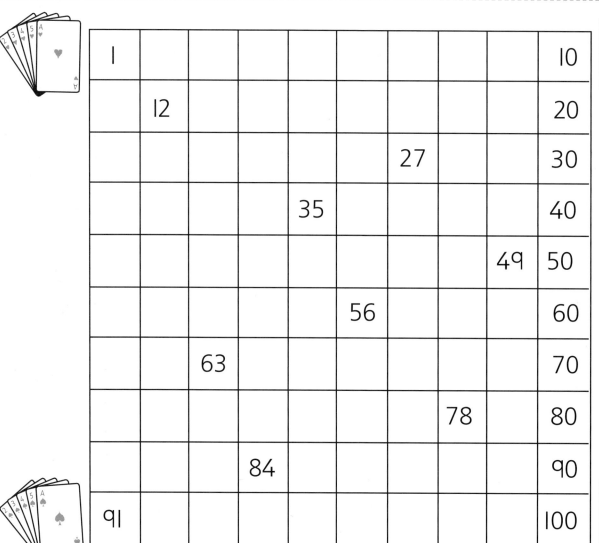

1									10
	12								20
						27			30
			35						40
								49	50
					56				60
		63							70
							78		80
			84						90
91									100

4.2   Make a 2-digit number

 2–4

What you need

- game board per child
- set of 0–9 number cards per child
- about ten counters per child

What to do

- Give each child a set of number cards and a game board. Children shuffle all the number cards together and place them face down in a pile in the middle of the table.
- Each child draws a card from the pack and places it in either column on their game board. Once placed, a number card cannot be moved. Each child then takes another card and puts it in the other column to make a 2-digit number. The child who has made the largest number is the winner of that round and takes a counter.
- The digit cards are removed from the game board, the cards are reshuffled and play continues.
- The winner is the first child to collect ten counters.

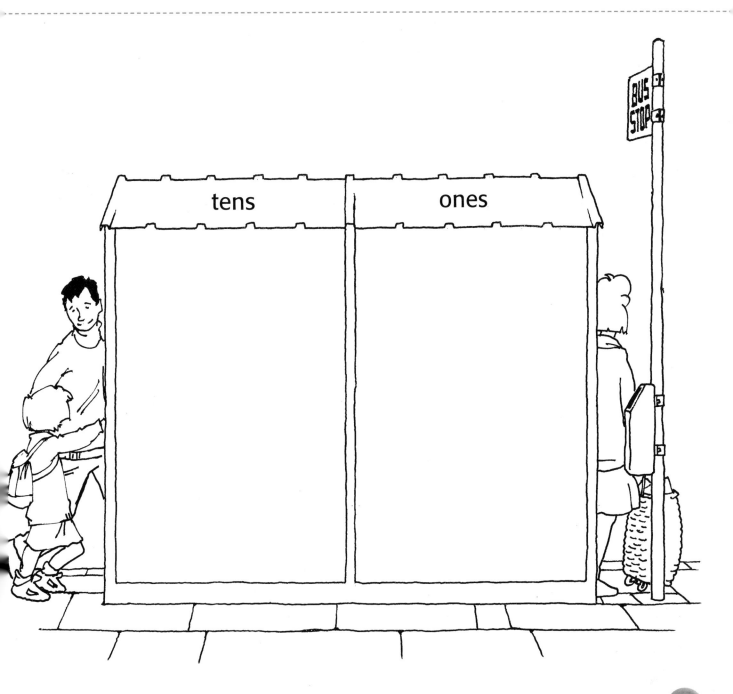

tens   ones

BUS STOP

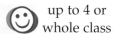

4.3 ▷ I've got the tens and units

up to 4 or
whole class

- game board per child (page 13)
- set of cards
- five counters per child
- different coloured pencil per child

What to do

- The game cards are shuffled and placed in a pile face down.
- Each child colours in any five numbers on their game board.
- The caller, or teacher, chooses a card and reads aloud the clue in words. They do not read the number in the circle.
- The children listen to the clues and try to find the number on their game board. If the number is coloured, they place a counter on it.
- The first child to cover all of his or her five numbers shouts *Stop!* The caller then checks the numbers covered against the cards used.
- The winner becomes the new caller.

Variation
Children colour more than five numbers.

four tens and five units (45)	seven tens and three units (73)	one ten and two units (12)	six tens and eight units (68)
seven tens and four units (74)	three tens and one unit (31)	three tens and no units (30)	two tens and nine units (29)
eight tens and one unit (81)	five tens and four units (54)	six tens and seven units (67)	three tens and two units (32)
one ten and six units (16)	two tens and eight units (28)	eight tens and five units (85)	seven tens and nine units (79)
five tens and three units (53)	nine tens and seven units (97)	four tens and six units (46)	nine tens and no units (90)

4.4 ▶ Place value loop

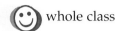 whole class

What you need

- set of cards, enlarged to A3 if possible

What to do

- Distribute all the cards among the children (some children may have more than one).
- Ask the children to read the card(s) quietly to themselves and to think about the tens and units in their number.
- Choose one child to start. That child reads out their question, for example, *Who has 5 tens and 3 units?*
- The child who has the answer reads out their card:

> I have **53**
>
> Who has **6 tens and I unit?**

- The game continues in this way until all the cards have been used.

Variation

Children can play in groups of six or more. Children distribute the cards and the same rules apply as above.

I have 26 Who has **5 tens and 3 units?**	**I have 53** Who has **6 tens and I unit?**
I have 6I Who has **0 tens and 8 units?**	**I have 8** Who has **3 tens and 7 units?**
I have 37 Who has **8 tens and 5 units?**	**I have 85** Who has **9 tens and 4 units?**
I have 94 Who has **4 tens and 5 units?**	**I have 45** Who has **7 tens and 0 units?**
I have 70 Who has **I ten and I unit?**	**I have II** Who has **6 tens and 3 units?**

I have 63
Who has **4 tens and 0 units?**

I have 40 Who has **3** tens and **9** units?	**I have 39** Who has **4** tens and **8** units?
I have 48 Who has **7** tens and **6** units?	**I have 76** Who has **9** tens and **3** units?
I have 93 Who has **2** tens and **1** unit?	**I have 21** Who has **1** ten and **9** units?
I have 19 Who has **4** tens and **4** units?	**I have 44** Who has **8** tens and **2** units?
I have 82 Who has **6** tens and **9** units?	**I have 69** Who has **3** tens and **2** units?
I have 32 Who has **0** tens and **5** units?	**I have 5** Who has **3** tens and **4** units?
I have 34 Who has **5** tens and **6** units?	**I have 56** Who has **9** tens and **7** units?
I have 97 Who has **6** tens and **5** units?	**I have 65** Who has **4** tens and **2** units?
I have 42 Who has **2** tens and **8** units?	**I have 28** Who has **1** ten and **7** units?
I have 17 Who has **5** tens and **8** units?	**I have 58** Who has **7** tens and **5** units?
I have 75 Who has **8** tens and **3** units?	**I have 83** Who has **2** tens and **6** units?

5.1 ▶ Correct order number cards

 2

What you need

- record sheet
- set of 0–50 number cards
- pencil per child

What to do

- Children shuffle the cards and place them face down in the middle of the table.
- One child is Player 1 and the other is Player 2. One child chooses a card. Both children decide in which box to write the number. Children take turns to choose three more cards. Once a number has been written down, it cannot be changed. The children are aiming to write the numbers in order from smallest to largest.
- The winner of the round is the child whose numbers are written in order, smallest to largest (or has more numbers in order, smallest to largest). They write their player number in the Winner box.
- Play continues for ten rounds. The overall winner is the child who has won more rounds.

Variation

↑ Use a set of 0–100 number cards.

	Player 1	Player 2	Winner
1.			
2.			
3.			
4.			
5.			
6.			
7.			
8.			
9.			
10.			

5.2 ▷ Number tiles

 2–4

What you need

- game board, enlarged to A3 if possible
- set of 1–100 number cards (cut out from the enlarged game board) in an envelope

What to do

- Children take turns to shake the envelope containing the number cards. Then, without looking, they each take seven from the envelope and hide these from their opponents.
- Each child takes a turn to place one of their seven number cards on its matching number on the game board.
- In subsequent turns, children must place a number card so that it touches any other number card already on the game board. The cards may touch vertically, horizontally or diagonally. If they cannot place a card on the game board, they take a new card from the envelope.
- The winner is the first child to get rid of all their cards.

Variations

↑ Use a blank 100 square (page 18).
- Add two blank number cards to the set of 1–100 cards. The blanks can be placed on any square, with the child saying the number.
↓ Use only part of the board, for example, 1–50 and only the 1–50 number cards.
- The winner is the first child to cover four numbers that make a square.

1	2	3	4	5	6	7	8	9	10
11	12	13	14	15	16	17	18	19	20
21	22	23	24	25	26	27	28	29	30
31	32	33	34	35	36	37	38	39	40
41	42	43	44	45	46	47	48	49	50
51	52	53	54	55	56	57	58	59	60
61	62	63	64	65	66	67	868	69	70
71	72	73	74	75	76	77	78	79	80
81	82	83	84	85	86	87	88	89	90
91	92	93	94	95	96	97	98	99	100

5.3 **100 square pictures** 1

What you need

- 100 square (page 17)
- coloured pencil
- 100 square picture numbers

What to do

- Provide each child with a 100 square and one of the sets of numbers below.
- Children colour each of the numbers to make a picture/pattern.

Variation

↑ Children use a blank 100 square (page 18).

Answers

a

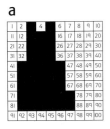

b

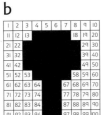

c

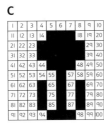

d

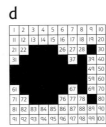

e

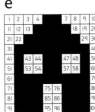

f

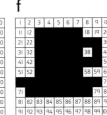

---

a

3	14	5	46	77	13	82
24	15	23	56	87	34	86
33	44	83	25	52	45	
73	75	84	62	66	35	
43	64	55	42	54	76	
53	63	74	65	85	72	

b

95	48	16	44	65	57
24	35	54	34	75	38
47	66	85	37	86	36
76	45	26	14	27	96
23	55	15	56	25	
43	28	46	17	33	

c

24	68	84	16	28	76
78	56	26	88	74	97
15	46	47	25	17	34
37	86	38	36	45	35
64	95	27	66	96	

d

25	57	38	32	64	48	66
43	33	63	45	34	62	42
24	46	68	56	53	41	29
75	58	74	47	79	55	36
51	52	23	65	73	44	35
54						

e

14	35	36	17	23	93	26
77	46	6	68	62	33	88
65	45	15	5	28	79	32
99	69	42	38	97	52	34
55	82	37	92	16	94	67
24	59	66	83	56	87	73
89	25	78	39	74	63	49
72	84	27	64	98		

f

13	74	67	76	53	68
29	39	47	24	46	61
27	43	28	37	69	48
23	36	64	73	49	16
55	63	54	33	26	15
44	25	75	14	45	56
57	72	17	62	77	65
34	66	78	35		

5.4 100 square puzzles

 1

What you need

- paper and pencil

What to do

- Draw the following on the board for children to copy. Ask them to complete the missing numbers from a 100 square.

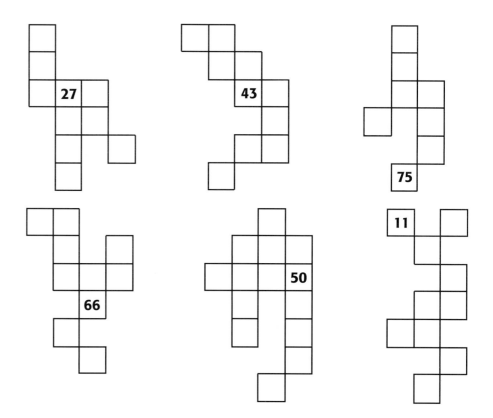

Answers

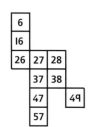 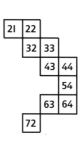 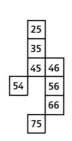 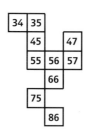 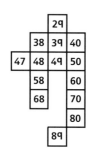 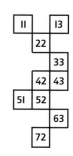

5.5 Order the children

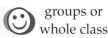 groups or whole class

What you need

- Post-it note per child, each with a different number between 0 and 100 on it

What to do

- Stick a different number onto each child's back.
- The children walk around asking each child they meet a yes/no question to try to work out their number, for example *Am I bigger than 50? Do I have seven tens?*
- When the children have worked out their numbers, they position themselves in order, smallest to largest.

5.1 ▸ Match the facts

 2

What you need

- set of addition and corresponding subtraction number facts to 10 cards, for example, for 7:

$7 - 0 = 7$	$0 + 7 = 7$
$7 - 1 = 6$	$1 + 6 = 7$
$7 - 2 = 5$	$2 + 5 = 7$

etc.

What to do

- Children shuffle the cards and spread them out face down in the middle of the table.
- They then take turns to choose two cards. If the cards state a matching addition and subtraction fact, i.e. $7 - 1 = 6$ and $6 + 1 = 7$ (or $1 + 6 = 7$) they keep them; if not, they are placed back in their original positions on the table.
- When all the cards have been chosen, the children count how many cards they have. The winner is the child with more cards.

Variations

- Use any addition and subtraction number facts to 10 cards.
- ↑ Use addition and subtraction number facts for two numbers, for example 6 and 7.

5.2 ▸ Give me the inverse

 2

What you need

- set of 1–20 number cards

What to do

- Shuffle the cards and place them face down in the centre of the table. One child takes two cards and uses them to make an addition calculation. For example, if they take 18 and 6, the calculation would be $18 + 6 = 24$.
- The other child then gives a corresponding subtraction fact, for example $24 - 6 = 18$. If they do this correctly, they take the cards; otherwise, the first child keeps them.
- The winner is the child with more number cards when they have all been used.

Variation

The first child makes a subtraction calculation and the second makes the corresponding addition calculation.

5.3 ▸ To the board

 whole class

What you need

- board

What to do

- Mark the board in two sections. Divide the class into two teams and seat each in a line.
- Write an addition fact up to 20 on the board. The first child from each team comes to the board and writes a corresponding subtraction fact. For example, if you write $15 + 3 = 18$, they write $18 - 3 = 15$ or $18 - 15 = 3$. Teams get a point for a correct calculation and the first child to complete one gains an extra point for their team. Both children then go and sit at the end of their line.
- Continue until each child has had a turn. The winners are the team with the most points.

Variations

- Write subtraction facts or a mixture of addition and subtraction facts.

7.1 ▷ Cover the stars

 2

What you need

- game board per child
- two 1–6 number dice
- 40 counters

What to do

- Each child takes a turn to roll both dice and add the two numbers.
- Using their counters each child then covers up one, two or three numbers that, when added together, equal the total number of both dice. For example, if a child's dice total 11, she or he can choose to cover up 1 and 10; or 5, 2 and 4; or any combination that totals 11.
- The children continue taking turns rolling the dice and covering up numbers until a total cannot be found. Each child then adds together remaining uncovered numbers and the total is their score.
- The winner is the child with the lowest score.

Variations

↑ Children can only cover up two numbers.
↑ Children can only cover up three numbers.
- The winner is the first child to cover all their numbers.

.2 > Add or subtract balloons

 2

What you need

- game board per child
- two 1–6 number dice
- 24 counters

What to do

- Children take turns to roll the dice.
- With each roll, a child has two choices in determining which number to cover on the game board: they can either add the two numbers together, or subtract the smaller number from the larger number. If the child cannot cover a number on their game board, they miss a turn.
- The winner is the first child to cover all the numbers on their game board.

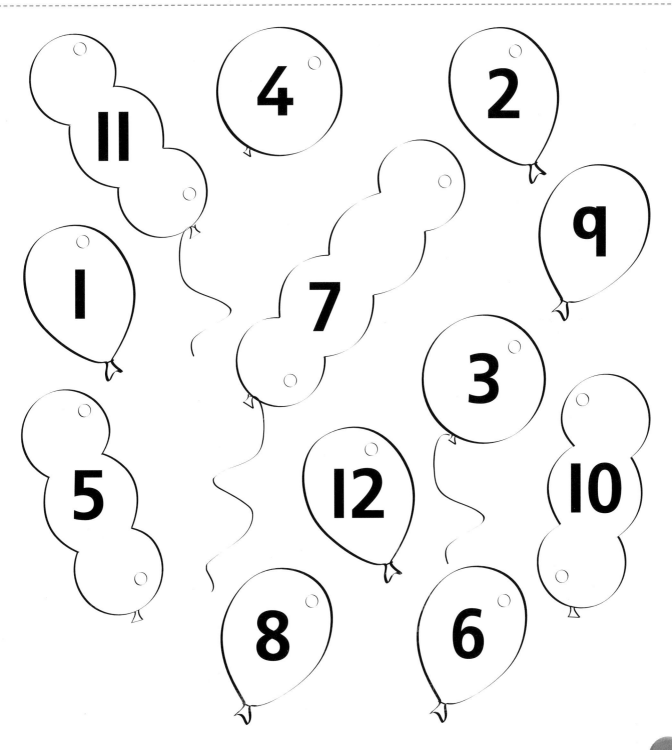

7.3 > Make a line

 2

What you need

- game board
- two 1–6 number dice
- 50 counters (25 of one colour, 25 of another)

What to do

- One child places one of their counters on the Start at the bottom of the page, to move up the page. The other child places one of their counters on the Start at the left of the page, to move across the page.
- Children take turns to roll both dice and subtract the smaller number from the larger number to find the difference. (If a child rolls a double, they roll again.) They place that number of counters, one after the other, in the squares on the game board connecting them to the starting counter. The line formed does not have to be a straight line but there can be no skipped boxes or diagonal moves. If a child comes across an opponent's counter or a black square blocking their path, they must go around it.
- The winner is the first child to form an unbroken line of counters from one side of the game board to the other.

7.4 ▷ Number line difference

 2

What you need

- 0–10 number line
- 0–9 die
- two counters per child

What to do

- Children take turns to roll the die twice, each time moving one of their counters that number of steps along the number line. For example, throw a 6 and move one counter 6 places. Then throw a 2 and move the second counter 2 places. They then work out the difference between the numbers covered by their counters (4). That is their score for that round. The counters are returned to zero.
- When each child has had five turns, they add up their total scores. The winner is the child with the higher total.

7.5 ▷ In a minute

 2–4

What you need

- timer
- 0–9 die

What to do

- One child throws the die and sets the timer for one minute.
- Working individually, children write as many calculations as they can with the answer shown by the die.
- When the minute is up, they compare answers. The winner of that round is the child with most correct calculations (as agreed by the group). The winner rolls the die to start the next round.
- The winner is the child who has won most rounds after a set time or number of rounds.

7.6 ▷ Ping-pong facts

 2

What you need

- paper and pencil per child

What to do

- Children decide who is going to serve first. The server says a number from 1 to 10 and the other child gives an addition or subtraction fact with this answer. For example, if the server says 7, the second child may respond with *5 plus 2*. The server writes this down. If the suggested fact gives the correct answer, the server picks another number. If the fact gives the wrong answer, or the second child repeats a fact they have already said, they *Stop* and swap roles.
- When each child has served five times, the children count up the number of correct facts written down. The winner is the child who said more.

Variations

- The server says an addition or subtraction fact, written on cards if necessary, and the other child responds with the answer.
- Children can play with a third child as the umpire who writes down the facts. After each game, the umpire swaps with one of the players.

7.7 ▷ Addition and subtraction bingo

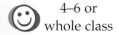 4–6 or whole class

What you need

- one game board per child
- 12 counters per child
- set of 0–10 number cards

What to do

- Provide each child with one game board and twelve counters.
- The caller (or teacher) shuffles the 0–10 number cards and places them in a pile face down in front of them.
- The caller takes the top card in the pile and calls it out to the class, for example 6. Each child looks to find a matching addition or subtraction calculation on their game board, for example 2 + 4 or 10 – 4. If a child finds a match, they put a counter over the calculation. Children can only cover one calculation each go.
- The winner is the first child to get three counters in a row vertically, horizontally or diagonally and call out *Bingo!* If the caller goes through all the number cards without any child calling bingo, they should reshuffle the cards and continue playing until someone has won.

Variations

- The winner is the first child to cover all their numbers.
- Provide children with two or more game boards.

1 + 0	7 – 0	9 + 1
9 – 1	4 – 3	7 – 3
5 + 3	6 + 0	10 – 0
1 + 8	8 – 2	1 + 1

3 + 0	10 – 7	4 + 0
2 – 0	10 – 1	5 – 5
8 – 6	0 + 10	0 + 5
0 + 0	8 – 3	2 + 5

1 + 4	9 – 0	4 + 2
8 – 8	5 – 0	7 – 6
7 – 1	3 + 6	3 + 0
8 + 2	2 – 2	2 + 2

0 + 0	8 – 5	2 + 0
5 + 4	4 – 0	5 – 3
10 – 2	6 + 2	10 – 3
0 + 1	10 – 0	5 + 2

7 + 2	5 – 4	5 + 5
9 – 4	3 + 3	8 – 1
2 + 1	10 – 0	0 + 0
2 + 6	9 – 7	6 – 3

0 + 7	9 – 3	2 + 0
4 + 1	10 – 1	8 – 0
3 – 1	0 + 1	8 – 4
6 + 4	0 – 0	2 + 2

10 – 4	0 + 4	1 + 1
3 + 0	2 + 4	9 – 0
7 – 7	10 – 0	0 + 6
1 + 0	8 – 0	6 + 5

1 – 1	2 + 3	4 + 4
10 – 5	0 + 0	9 – 2
2 + 7	7 – 4	7 + 3
9 – 5	7 + 0	4 – 2

3 + 1	3 – 0	8 + 1
9 – 0	1 + 0	10 – 3
8 + 0	6 – 0	1 + 2
3 – 3	7 + 1	9 – 1

4 + 6	0 + 0	10 – 0
7 – 5	9 – 9	5 + 1
4 + 3	0 + 2	8 – 7
5 – 1	6 – 1	3 + 2

6 – 2	10 – 0	0 + 0
5 + 0	1 + 5	8 – 1
5 – 2	7 – 2	2 + 8
0 + 1	6 + 1	3 – 2

9 – 8	3 + 5	9 – 0
1 + 3	10 – 2	2 + 1
1 + 9	0 + 2	4 – 1
10 – 10	6 – 4	4 + 5

7.8 ▷ Say it and you're out

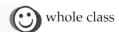 whole class

What you need

- no resources needed

What to do

- Write any four numbers from 0–10 on the board, for example 2, 5, 7 and 10, and ask the children to stand behind their chairs.
- Ask the first child an addition calculation, for example, *Four add four?* If the answer is not one of the numbers on the board, the child stays in, and chooses another child for you to ask a different addition question. If the answer is one of the numbers on the board (for example, *Three add seven?*), then the child has to sit down. Start again with a different child.
- Continue going around the class asking quick-fire addition calculations until one child is left in. This child is the winner.

Variations

↑ Use subtraction facts or both addition and subtraction facts.
- Use addition and/or subtraction number fact cards.

7.9 ▷ Addition lottery

 whole class

What you need

- paper and pencil per child

What to do

- Ask each child to write down any five numbers from 0 to 10.
- Give addition calculations to 10, for example, *Four plus two?* Children do not call out the answer but rather they work it out quietly. If it is one of their five lottery numbers, they cross it off. (Remember to keep a record of all the calculations for checking purposes.)
- Continue asking other addition calculation questions to 10. The winner is the first child to cross off all their numbers.

Variations

- Play 'Subtraction lottery'.
↑ Play 'Addition and subtraction lottery'.

7.10 ▷ Coin combinations

 1

What you need

- paper and pencil
- selection of small coins

What to do

- Write the following on the board for children to copy and complete.
  How many combinations of coins
  can you find that make 11p?

Variation

↓↑ Change the amount to any value.

7.11 > **Magic number puzzles** 1

What you need

- paper and pencil

What to do

- Draw the following magic number puzzles on the board for the children to copy and complete.
- Ask the children if they can find more than one way to complete each puzzle.

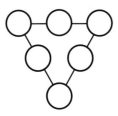

Use all the numbers I to 6.
Make the total of each row 9.
Variations: Make the total of each row 10/11/12.

Use all the numbers I to 8.
Make the total of each row 12.
Variations: Make the total of each row 13/14/15.

Use all the numbers I to 9.
Each row horizontally, vertically and diagonally must add up to 15.

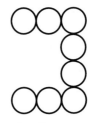

Use all the numbers I to 8.
Each row horizontally and vertically must add up to 15.
Variations: Make the total of each row 13/16.

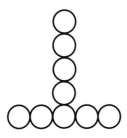

Use all the numbers I to 9.
Each row horizontally and vertically must add up to 27.
Variations: Make the total of each row 23/24/25/26.

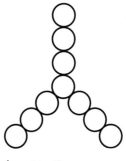

Use all the numbers I to 10.
Each row must add up to 23.
Variations: Make the total of each row 19/21.

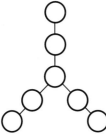

Use all the numbers I to 7.
Make the total of each row 10.
Variations: Make the total of each row 12/14.

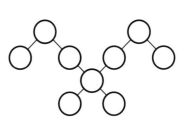

Use all the numbers I to 9.
Make the total of each row 15.

8.1 ▶ Lu-Lu: a variation on a Polynesian adding game 2–4

What you need

- Four Lu-Lu stones (large counters: one side of each counter is blank, the other sides are as follows)

- paper and pencil per child
- ten counters per child

What to do

- Children take turns to roll or spin the Lu-Lu stones and find the total of the dots showing, writing the answer on their sheet of paper.
- Any stone that falls blank side up is rolled by the next child as a bonus. For example, if the first child rolls a 2, a 3 and two blanks, their score is 5. The second child rolls the two blank stones, records the resulting total, then takes their regular turn with all four stones, and combines both totals to get their score for the round. Any blanks rolled as a bonus do not entitle the next child to roll extra stones.
- For each round the child with the highest total collects a counter.
- The overall winner of the game is the first child to collect ten counters.

Variations

- Use three stones marked with 1, 2 and 3 dots.
- Use five stones marked with 1, 2, 3, 4 and 5 dots.
- Eliminate the bonus.

8.2 ▶ Same calculation? 2

What you need

- addition number fact cards for 5 and 6

What to do

- Children shuffle the cards and spread them out face down in the middle of the table.
- They then take turns to choose two cards. If the cards say the same addition calculation but in a different order, for example, 3 + 2 and 2 + 3, and the child can say the correct answer, they keep both cards.
- If the cards do not say the same addition calculation, for example, 3 + 2 and 1 + 4, they are replaced in their original position on the table.
- When all the cards have been chosen, the children count how many cards they have. The winner is the child with more cards.

Variation

↑ Use addition number fact cards for 7 and 8, 9 and 10 or any other combinations.

8.3 ▶ Make the number 1

What you need

- paper and pencil

What to do

- Draw the following on the board for children to copy and complete.
- Ask the children if they can find more than one way to complete each one.

What 4 numbers added together total 6?

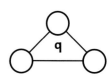

What 3 numbers added together total 9?

.4   Magic squares

 1

What you need

- paper and pencil

What to do

- Draw the following magic squares on the board for children to copy and complete. All the rows and columns for each square should have the same total.

	1	
3	5	
	9	

		9
	7	8
5		

11	3	
7	8	
	13	

Answers

8	1	6
3	5	7
4	9	2

10	2	9
6	7	8
5	12	4

11	3	10
7	8	9
6	13	5

.5   Cross additions

 1

What you need

- paper and pencil

What to do

- Write the following puzzles on the board.

Sum of 8

Sum of 9

Sum of 10

- The children copy and complete each puzzle, using the numbers 1 to 5 to make the sum of the column and the row the same.

Variations

↑ Use the numbers 1 to 7 to complete these puzzles.

Sum of 15

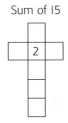

Sum of 17

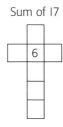

Sum of ?

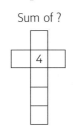

↑ Use the numbers 1 to 9 to complete these puzzles.

Sum of 27

Sum of ?

Sum of 23

Sum of 25

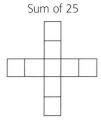

9.1 ▷ Add the number thrown

 2

What you need

- set of cards
- 1–6 number die
- 16 counters
- paper and pencil per child

What to do

- Children shuffle the cards and place them face down in a pile in the middle of the table.
- Child A turns over a card, for example, 'Add the number thrown 4 times', and rolls the die, for example to show 5. Child A then writes down the appropriate addition calculation, i.e. 5 + 5 + 5 + 5 = 20, and the appropriate multiplication calculation, i.e. 4 × 5 = 20.
- Child B then repeats the activity, choosing a new card, rolling the die and writing down the corresponding addition and multiplication calculations.
- The child with the higher score takes a counter. If the scores are the same, both children take a counter.
- The game continues until all the cards have been used. The winner is the child with more counters.

Variation

Use a 0–9 die.

Add the number thrown twice	Add the number thrown twice	Add the number thrown twice	Add the number thrown twice
Add the number thrown **3** times	Add the number thrown **3** times	Add the number thrown **3** times	Add the number thrown **3** times
Add the number thrown **4** times	Add the number thrown **4** times	Add the number thrown **4** times	Add the number thrown **4** times
Add the number thrown **5** times	Add the number thrown **5** times	Add the number thrown **5** times	Add the number thrown **5** times

.2 > Draw an array 2

What you need

- 2, 4, 6, 8, 10 number cards
- squared paper per child
- coloured pencils

What to do

- Children shuffle the cards and place them face down in a pile in the middle of the table.
- They then take turns to choose a card, for example 8.
- Each child colours in a block of squares to match the number thrown, as shown. They then write a multiplication calculation to match the block coloured, i.e. 2 × 4 or 4 × 2.
- Children continue, reshuffling the cards as necessary. The winner is the child who fits more blocks on their piece of paper.

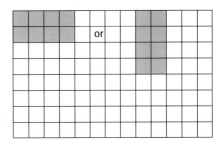

.3 > Write the calculation 2

What you need

- squared paper
- ruler
- different coloured pencil per child

What to do

- Child A draws a rectangle on the squared paper in their colour.
- Child B counts the number of rows and the number of squares in each row, recording the resulting multiplication calculation, as shown.
- If the calculation is correct, Child B draws a rectangle for Child A to record as a multiplication; if not Child A draws another rectangle for Child B to record.

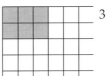

$3 \times 2 = 6$

- The winner is the child with more rectangles in their colour when they have filled the paper.

Variation

Children use pegs and a peg-board or elastic bands and a Geoboard instead of paper and pencils.

.4 > The array game 2

What you need

- 20 counters per child
- paper and pencil per child

What to do

- Child A takes a handful of their counters (an even number), counts them and tells their opponent how many there are, for example, 12.
- Using their own counters, Child B then makes this into an array, for example:

- Child B then lists this as a multiplication calculation, for example $3 \times 4 = 12$.
- The game continues with children alternating roles. The winner is the child with more different calculations after a predetermined time.

10.1 ▶ Double and half

 2

What you need

- set of cards

What to do

- Children shuffle the cards and spread them out face down in the middle of the table.
- Children take turns to choose two cards. If the cards show a question and the correct answer, for example, 'Twice 6' and '12', the child keeps both cards. If the cards do not match they are placed back in their original position on the table.
- When all the cards have been chosen, the children count how many cards they have. The winner is the child with more cards.

Variation

Photocopy the number cards and the question cards onto different coloured card. Children choose one of each colour and see if they match.

2	14	50	**Twice 6**	20 ÷ 2
4	16	60	**Twice 9**	**Half of 4**
6	18	100	**Twice 30**	**Half of 40**
8	20	**Double 50**	4 × 2	**Half of 12**
10	30	**Double 7**	8 × 2	$\frac{1}{2}$ **of 8**
12	40	**Double 20**	100 ÷ 2	$\frac{1}{2}$ **of 60**

0.2 ▷ Doubling game

 2–4

What you need

- game board
- 1–6 number die
- different coloured counter per child

What to do

- Children place their counter on Start.
- Each child takes turns to roll the die and move their counter the corresponding number of spaces.
- The child must then double the number their counter lands on. If the group agrees that their answer is correct, they move their counter on one space. If it is incorrect, they move their counter back one space.
- The winner is the first child to reach or pass Finish.

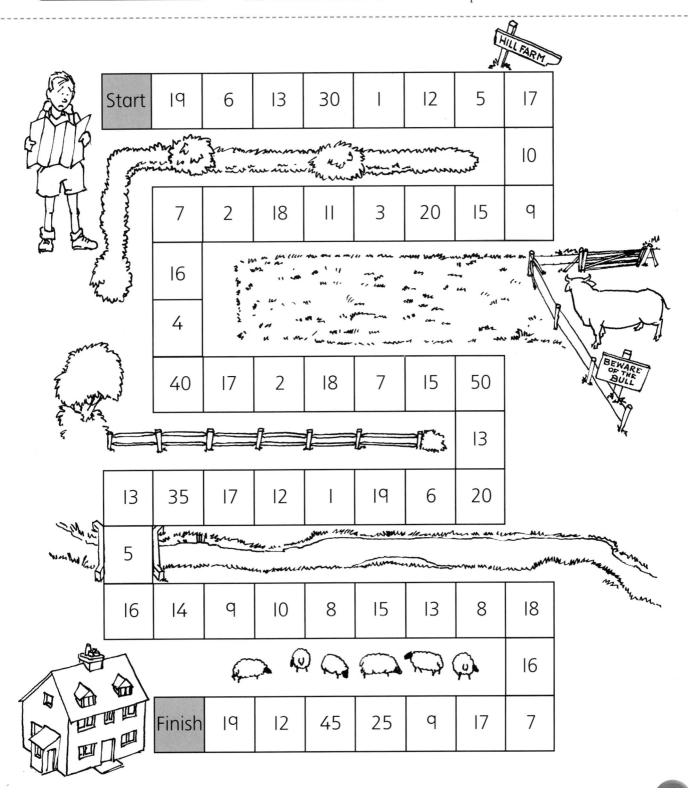

10.3 ▷ Halving game 2–4

What you need

- game board
- 1–6 number die
- different coloured counter per child

What to do

- Children place their counter on Start.
- Each child takes turns to roll the die and move their counter the corresponding number of spaces.
- The child then halves the number they land on. If the group agrees that their answer is correct, they move their counter on one space. If it is incorrect, they move their counter back one space.
- The winner is the first child to reach or pass Finish.

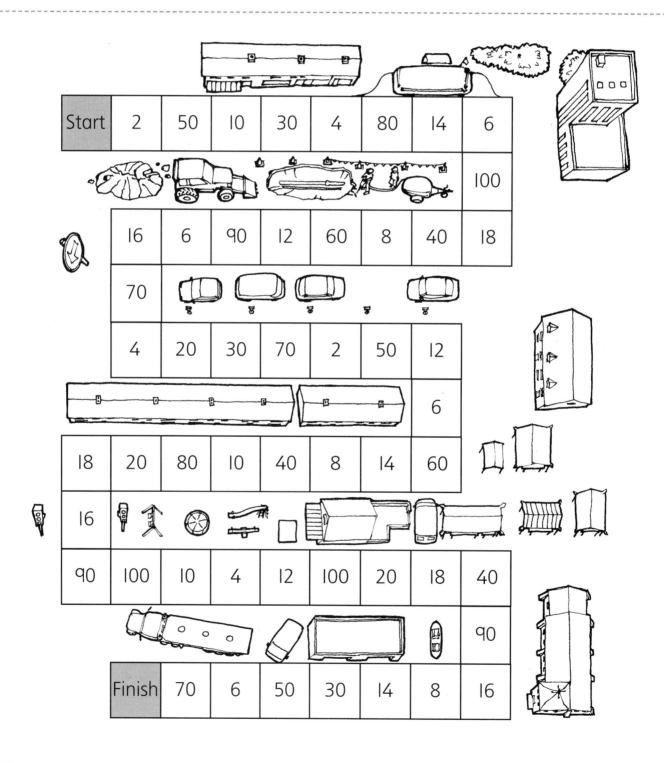

10.4 Forward, double, back 2–4

What you need

- 100 square (page 17), enlarged to A3 if possible
- two 1–6 number dice
- different coloured counter per child

What to do

- Each child places their counter on 1.
- Children take turns to roll the two dice. On their turn, the child looks at the dice and decides which shows the highest number. They then double the value of that die and move their counter forwards that number of places on the 100 square. (If a child rolls a double, they roll again until they get two different numbers.) The child then moves their counter back the number of spaces indicated by the other die.
- Play continues until one child reaches 100.

Variations

↓ Children do not move their counter back the number of spaces shown on the die with the lowest number.
- The winner is the child who has progressed furthest after each player has had five turns.

10.5 Double up  whole class

What you need

- 1–6 number die

What to do

- Divide the children into two teams, Team A and Team B. Ask the children in each team to stand in a line, one behind the other.
- Give the first child in Team A a number, for example 3. That child then doubles it (6). Play then passes to the first child in Team B who doubles the number again (12).
- Play continues alternating between the two teams, each time going to the next child in the line. If a child says an incorrect double, their team's turn stops there and the other team scores a point. Play then begins again with the next child in Team B and a different number.
- The game ends when each child in both teams has had a turn. The winners are the team with the most points.

Variation

Give the children a larger number to halve. If the team reaches the smallest whole number (for example, 24, 12, 6, 3), they score a point.

10.6 Twice as much 1

What you need

- paper and pencil

What to do

- Draw the following on the board for children to copy.

- Children write the numbers 1 to 6 in the ovals to make the total of the numbers in the large oval twice the total of the numbers in the small oval. (There is more than one possible solution.)

Variation

↑ Children use each of numbers 1 to 7 only once to make the total of the first oval three times the total of the second.

11.1 ▷ Multiplication tic-tac-toe

 2

What you need

- game board
- 0–9 die
- die labelled: 2, 2, 2, 10, 10, 10
- 40 counters (20 of one colour, 20 of another)

What to do

- Children take turns to roll the dice and multiply the two numbers together.
- They then find the product of these two numbers on the game board and place one of their counters over it. If a child's answer is a number that has already been covered, they miss a turn.
- The game continues until one child covers four numbers in a row (vertically, horizontally or diagonally).

Variations

- The winner is the child with more counters on the game board once all the numbers are covered or after a predetermined time.
- Each child has a game board.

6	60	6	18	2	10
40	8	10	80	0	12
0	2	60	30	40	14
4	90	30	70	20	90
8	14	20	50	4	10
80	0	12	70	50	16

1.2 First to cover

 2

What you need

- 2 times-table game board per child (page 40)
- 0–9 die
- 40 counters (20 of one colour, 20 of another)

What to do

- Children take turns to throw the die.
- On their turn, the child multiplies the number thrown by 2. They then find the corresponding number on their game board and place one of their counters on it. If a number already has a counter on it, the child misses a turn.
- The winner is the first child to cover all the numbers on their game board.

Variation

Use the 10 times-tables game board (page 40).

1.3 Stack them up

 2

What you need

- 2 times-table game board (page 40)
- 0–9 number die
- 40 counters (20 of one colour, 20 of another)

What to do

- Children take turns to throw the die.
- On their turn, the child multiplies the number thrown by 2. They then place one of their counters in the space beside the corresponding number on the game board. If there is already a counter in the space (either one of their counters or one of their opponents), then the child places one of their coloured counters on top. That pile of counters then belongs to that child.
- The game continues in this way until both children have placed all their counters on the game board.
- Each child then carefully removes all the piles where the top counter is their colour. They count how many counters they have altogether. The winner is the child with more counters.

Variation

Use the 10 times-tables game board (page 40).

2 times-table

8		6	
0		10	
16		2	
4		18	
12		14	

10 times-table

80		50	
0		10	
60		20	
40		90	
70		30	

1.4   Know the facts

 2

What you need

- set of 0–9 number cards
- 20 counters

What to do

- Children shuffle the cards and place them face down in a pile. They take turns to turn over the top card.
- Both children multiply the number revealed by 2. The first child to say the answer takes a counter. When all the cards have been used, they are reshuffled and the game continues.
- When all 20 counters have been used, the children count how many counters they have. The winner is the child with more counters.

Variation
Children multiply by 10.

1.5   Whole class multiplication

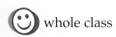 whole class

What you need

- 0–9 die

What to do

- Write × 2 on the board
- Throw the die and ask children to multiply the number thrown by 2 in their heads.
- Choose a child to give the answer. If they are correct, they nominate the child to give the next answer.
- Repeat, quickening the pace.

Variations
- Write × 10 on the board.
- Ask children to show their answer using digit cards/fans.

1.6   Three in a row

 2–4

What you need

- multiples of 2 and 10 from a set of 1–100 number cards (for example 2, 4, 6 … up to 20 and 10, 20, 30 …)

What to do

- Shuffle the cards and place them face down in a pile in the centre.
- Children take turns to take a card from the top of the pile. If they can say a corresponding tables fact, they keep the card; if not, they place it face up in the discard pile. For example, if a child picks up 10, they could say 1 times 10 (or 10 times 1) or 2 times 5 (or 5 times 2).
- When each child has three cards, they can choose whether to keep the card they pick up and discard one of the cards in their hand, or to discard the card they pick up immediately. They should try to get three consecutive multiple cards in either times-table, for example 12, 14, 16 or 50, 60, 70. If they run out of cards to pick up, the discard pile can be shuffled and placed face down.
- The winner is the first child to get three cards in a row.

12.1 ▷ Loop problems

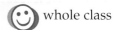 whole class

What you need

- set of cards, enlarged to A3 if possible

What to do

- Distribute all the cards among the children (some children may have more than one). Ask the children to read the card(s) quietly to themselves.
- Choose a child to start. That child reads the question on their card, for example, *In my Christmas stocking I found 16 nuts. If I eat 8, how many will I have left?*
- The child who has the card showing the answer reads out their card:

> **8**
> Dad shares **20** raisins between **5** children. How many raisins does each child get?

- The game continues in this way until all the cards have been used.

Variation

Children can play in groups of six or more. They distribute the cards and the same rules apply as above.

90 In my Christmas stocking I found **16** nuts. If I eat **8**, how many will I have left?	**8** Dad shares **20** raisins between **5** children. How many raisins does each child get?
4 At the cinema **14** tickets were sold. Another **5** people buy tickets. How many tickets have been sold altogether?	**19** **18** children are eating lunch. **6** finish and go out to play. How many children are left?
12 There are **13** apples. If **7** children take one each, how many are left?	**6** Mum works from **9** o'clock to **12** o'clock. How many hours does she work?
3 Alex climbs **8** stairs and then another **9** stairs to get to his bedroom. How many stairs does he climb altogether?	**17** There are **14** grapes on a bunch. I eat **7**. How many are left?
7 There are **10** lollipops between **2** children. How many does each child get?	**5** In his shop a baker has **5** trays. On each tray he has **7** cakes. How many cakes does the baker have altogether?

> **35**
> On Sunday we made **20** biscuits. By Wednesday **9** had been eaten. How many biscuits were left?

11 A piece of ribbon is **80** cm long. How many lengths of **8** cm can you cut from the ribbon?	**10** In our class **8** boys have dark hair and **7** boys have fair hair. How many boys are there altogether?
15 Charlie sent **12** invitations to his party. **3** children can't come. How many children will be coming?	**9** If **10** teams have **7** children each, how many children are there altogether?
70 Peter had **11** marbles. His friend gave him another **2**. How many marbles does he have now?	**13** During games the teacher made **10** teams of **6** children. How many children were there altogether?
60 Fabio had **17** football cards. He lost **3**. How many cards does he have now?	**14** Chris has **8** blue pencils and **8** red pencils. How many pencils does he have altogether?
16 There are **5** milk crates. Each crate holds **4** bottles. How many bottles are there altogether?	**20** 2 children have **20** pencils each. How many pencils altogether?
40 There are **5** tables in a classroom. **6** children sit at each table. How many children are in the classroom?	**30** 6 children share **12** stickers. How many does each child get?
2 A shopkeeper sells **15** loaves of bread in the morning and **10** in the afternoon. How many does he sell in a day?	**25** In a spelling test Toni and Jane got **50** marks each. How many did they get altogether?
100 Steve had **2** sandwiches for lunch. He ate both of them. How many sandwiches does he have left?	**0** For a party there were **70** balloons. **5** burst. How many balloons were left?
65 A rope is **100** cm long. How many lengths of **2** cm can you cut from it?	**50** There are **6** children sitting at a table. **5** of them are girls. How many are boys?
1 There are **40** boys, **20** girls and **9** teachers in the hall. How many people are in the hall altogether?	**69** A tank holds **10** fish. How many fish do **8** tanks hold?
80 There are **9** pairs of children working together. Each child has **1** pencil. How many pencils altogether?	**18** 10 teams have **9** players each. How many players altogether?

12.2 > Match the cards

 2

What you need

- set of cards, enlarged to A3 if possible

What to do

- Shuffle the cards and spread them out face down on the table.
- Children take turns to choose two cards. If the answers match, they keep them; if not, they are replaced in their original position on the table.
- The winner is the child with more cards when all the pairs have been collected.

Simon spent **50p** on a drink and **30p** on a packet of crisps. How much did he spend altogether?	Michael had **16** marbles. He lost **4**. How many does he have now?	Sarah had **20** sweets. She ate **5**. How many sweets does she have left?	Lisa had £l. She shares it with a friend. How much do they each get?
There are **5** tables in a classroom and **30** children. How many children sit at each table?	I buy **8** chews at **2p** each. How much change will I get from 20p?	**5** children eat **3** bananas each. How many do they eat altogether?	There are **2** teams with **10** children in each team. How many children altogether?
Sanjay had **20p**. He gave l5p to his best friend. How much money does Sanjay have now?	There are **6** red, **6** blue and **5** green pencils. How many pencils are there altogether?	David bought an orange for **20p**. How much change did he get from £l?	I have **20p**. I buy **5** sweets at **3p** each. How much change will I get?
There are **40** counters in groups of **4**. How many groups are there?	**5** families have **4** children each. How many children are there altogether?	John has **5** people in his family and so does Lea. How many people altogether?	There are **60** children in Year **2**. All the children are divided into teams of **10**. How many teams are there?
Sharon buys **2** lollipops at **25p** each. How much does she have to pay?	**4** children have **3** biscuits each. How many biscuits altogether?	Niyat had **20** stickers. She lost **3**. How many does she have now?	I have **30p**. I spend **26p**. How much change will I get?

12.3 ▶ Problem-solving game

 2

What you need

- game board
- set of cards (page 44), enlarged to A3 if possible
- 1–6 number die
- different coloured counter per child

What to do

- Children shuffle the cards and place them face down in a pile in the middle of the table. Each child places their counter on Start.
- Each child takes turns to roll the die and move their counter the corresponding number of spaces.
- That child then chooses a card and works out the answer. If their partner agrees that it is correct, they move their counter on one space. If it is incorrect, they move their counter back one space.
- The winner is the first child to reach or pass Finish.

Estimate, measure and compare lengths, masses and capacities, using standard units; suggest suitable units and equipment for such measurements. Read a simple scale to the nearest labelled division, including using a ruler to draw and measure lines to the nearest centimetre.

13.1 ▶ Going home

 2

What you need

- record sheet per child
- ruler per child
- 1–6 number die
- different coloured pencil per child

What to do

- Children take turns to roll the die. The child whose turn it is finds School on their record sheet and, using their ruler to measure, draws a straight line the number of centimetres shown on the die. For example, if the number rolled is 5, the measurement of the line will be 5 cm. The child colours in their path.
- The children may choose to travel any of the paths that lead to Home. If a child is unable to draw a straight line on the path, because the number thrown is too big, they miss a turn.
- The winner is the first child to reach Home.

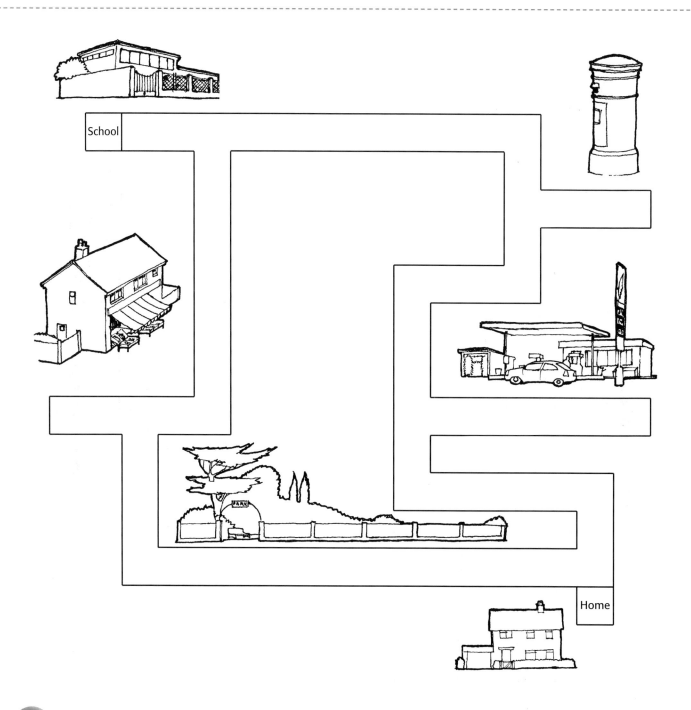

13.2 Which is longer?

 2

What you need

- eight equal-sized cards (from an A4 sheet of card) labelled A to I
- game board
- 40 counters

What to do

- Give each pair a copy of the game board. Shuffle the cards and place them in a pile, face down. Give each child 20 counters.
- Each child turns over a card and together they work out the difference in length between the two lines. The child with the shorter line gives the other child the corresponding number of counters. For example, if the first child takes C and the second G, the second gives the first one counter.
- When the cards have all been used, they are shuffled and placed face down again.
- The winner is the child with more counters after a predetermined time.

Variations

- The child with the longer line gives counters to the child with the shorter line.

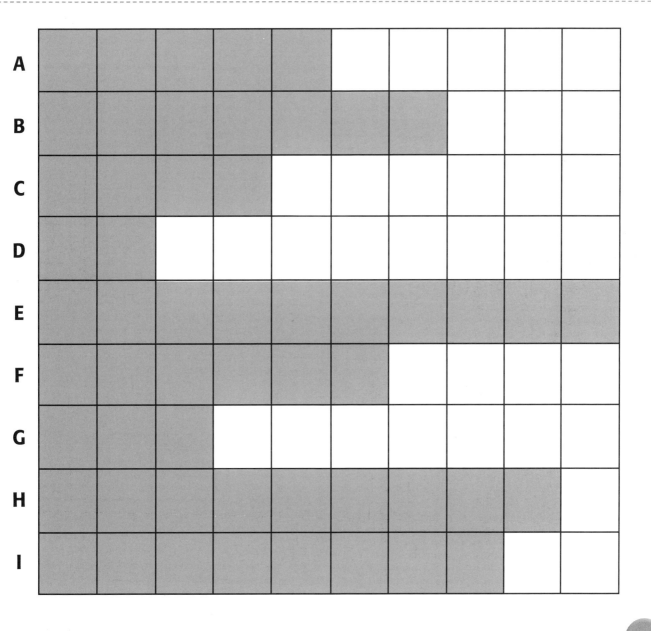

13.3 ▶ Estimate and measure my length 2–4

What you need

- five to ten straws of different lengths, each labelled A, B, C, etc.
- paper and pencil per child
- ruler
- five to ten counters

What to do

- Each child estimates the length of straw A in centimetres and writes it down. They then measure the length of the straw in centimetres.
- The child with the closest estimate takes a counter.
- The game continues with children measuring straw B, straw C and so on until all the straws have been used.
- The winner is the child with the most counters.

13.4 ▶ I spy 3–4 or whole class

What you need

- counters
- ruler

What to do

- One child looks around the classroom and chooses an object, saying *I spy with my little eye, something that is about [9] centimetres long*. The other children try to guess the object that the child is thinking about.
- The first child to guess the correct object measures it. If the actual length is within 5 centimetres of the estimated length, the child who chose it takes a counter. The child who guessed it chooses a different object and the game proceeds.
- The winner is the child who collects most counters.

Variation

↑ Use both centimetre and metre lengths.

13.5 ▶ Draw me a line whole class

What you need

- paper and pencil per child
- ruler per child

What to do

- Write a length such as 15 cm on the board.
- Children have to draw a straight line that they estimate to be 15 cm long.
- When they have done this, they check using a ruler and write down the actual length of the line they have drawn. The child who was closest chooses the next length for the class to draw.

3.6 More, less and exactly a kilogram 1

What you need

- paper and pencil
- balance and 1 kg weight, or scales

What to do

- Ask the children to estimate and write down ten things from around the classroom:
  - four that weigh more than 1 kg
  - four that weigh less than 1 kg
  - two that weigh exactly 1 kg.
- Give them time to find the objects, then ask them to weigh them and check their guesses. Did anyone identify all ten objects?

3.7 Estimate and measure the weight 2–4

What you need

- various objects in the classroom
- balance and weights
- counters

What to do

- Choose an object and ask the children to estimate its weight, first before picking it up and then after picking it up.
- Children then weigh the objects. The child with the closest estimate takes a counter.
- Children continue until all the objects have been estimated and weighed. The winner is the child with the most counters.

3.8 How many? 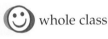 whole class

What you need

- clear plastic container half full of small cubes

What to do

- Show children the container half full of small cubes.

  Tell them how many cubes are in the container, for example, 60.
- Ask them to work out how many cubes would be needed to:
  a) fill the container   b) fill 2 containers   c) fill a container $\frac{1}{2}$ this size
  d) fill $\frac{1}{4}$ of this container   e) fill $1\frac{1}{2}$ containers   f) fill 10 containers.
- When the children have worked out the answers correctly, give them another set of numbers:
  a) ?   b) 160   c) 40   d) 20   e) 120   f) 800
  Tell them these are the answers to the same questions for a container of a different size. Can they find the missing number?

Variations

- Begin with a different number of cubes.
- Change the questions.
- Ask the children to estimate how many cubes they think are in the container, then answer the questions. When the children have done this they then count the number of cubes and answer the questions again, comparing the actual answers to their estimates.

14.1 Shapes and names

 2

What you need

- set of 2D shape label cards
- set of 2D shape cards (page 53)

What to do

- Children shuffle the cards and spread them out face down on the table. They take turns to choose two cards.
- If the cards match, they keep them. If the cards do not match they are placed back in their original position on the table.
- When all the cards have been chosen, the children count how many cards they have. The winner is the child with more cards.

Variation

Use a set of 3D shape label cards and a set of 3D shape cards (page 53).

2D shape label cards

square	**rectangle**
circle	**triangle**
pentagon	**hexagon**
octagon	

3D shape label cards

cube	**cuboid**
sphere	**cylinder**
cone	**pyramid**

2D shape cards

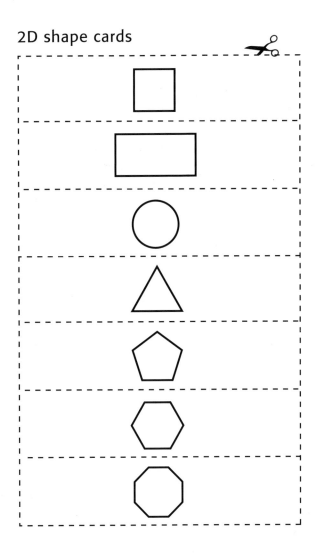

3D shape cards

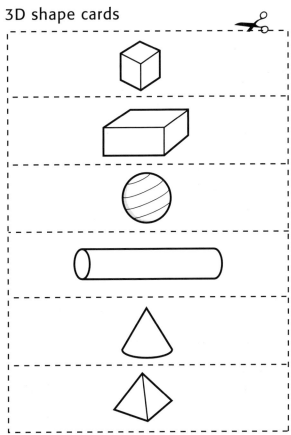

14.2 ▷ Name the shapes

 3–4

What you need

- selection of 3D shapes (about 20) of different sizes and colours in a tray
- tea towel
- paper and pencil per child

What to do

- Children study the shapes in the tray for one minute. The tray is then covered with the tea towel and each child writes down all the different shapes in the tray and their various attributes, for example, small red sphere.
- After a set time (say four minutes), remove the tea towel. Children then work out how many shapes they remembered.
- The child who remembered the greatest number of shapes then covers them again with the tea towel. The other children close their eyes and the child removes one object. They open their eyes and the tea towel is removed. The first child to spot which object has been removed takes the next turn at removing an object.

Variation
↓ Start with fewer shapes.

14.3 ▷ How many shapes?

 1

What you need

- paper and pencil

What to do

- Write on the board:
  How many triangles can you find in this shape?

Variations

- Change the shape, for example:

- How many squares can you find in this shape?

14.4 ▷ Matchsticks

 1

What you need

- pile of matchsticks

What to do

- Write the following on the board:
  Investigate different squares you can make.

4.5 > Sort the shapes

 2

What you need

- selection of 2D shapes (about 20) of different sizes and colours in a tray

What to do

- One child sorts the shapes using their own criteria.
- The other child has to guess the criteria. If they guess correctly, they take a shape of their choice.
- Children reverse roles and continue sorting the remaining shapes. The winner is the child with more shapes after a predetermined time.

Variation
Use a selection of 3D shapes.

4.6 > Describe the shapes

 groups of about 4

What you need

- selection of about 20 3D shapes in a feely bag

What to do

- Children take turns to choose a shape from the bag and describe some of its features by feeling, and not looking at it.
- The other children have to guess the name of the shape being described.
- When the shape has been guessed correctly, the child removes the shape from the bag to show the rest of the group.
- The child who guesses correctly chooses the next shape.

Variation
Use a selection of 2D shapes.

4.7 > Label the shapes

 2–4

What you need

- set of 3D shapes in a feely bag
- set of 3D shape label cards (page 52)
- feely bag

What to do

- Put the 3D shapes into the bag. Children take turns to select a card, then feel inside the bag to find the corresponding shape. If they pull out the correct shape, they keep it; if not, they return it to the bag.
- The winner is the child with most shapes when the bag is empty.

Variation
Use a selection of 2D shapes and a set of 2D shape label cards (page 52).

15.1 ▷ Collect the counters

 2

What you need

- game board
- different coloured counter per child
- 1–6 number die
- die labelled: up, down, left, right, joker, joker
- 60 counters

What to do

- Both children place their counters on Start. They take turns to roll both dice and move their counters accordingly. For example, one child might roll 4 and down. They then move their counter down four spaces. If they land on a space that says, for example, Collect 2 counters, then the child does so.
- If a child rolls a joker, they can decide whether to move up, down, left or right.
- The game continues in this way. The winner is the first child to collect 30 counters.

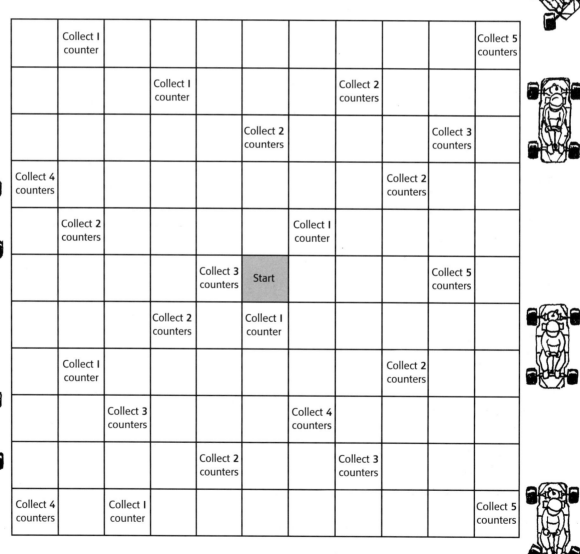

	Collect I counter										Collect 5 counters
		Collect I counter				Collect 2 counters					
			Collect 2 counters					Collect 3 counters			
Collect 4 counters							Collect 2 counters				
	Collect 2 counters				Collect I counter						
			Collect 3 counters	Start				Collect 5 counters			
		Collect 2 counters		Collect I counter							
	Collect I counter						Collect 2 counters				
		Collect 3 counters			Collect 4 counters						
			Collect 2 counters			Collect 3 counters					
Collect 4 counters		Collect I counter									Collect 5 counters

15.2 ▷ Class positions

 2–4

What you need

- game board
- 1–6 number die
- different coloured counter per child

What to do

- Children place their counters on Start. They take turns to roll the die and move their counter that number of spaces. If they land on a word or a phrase, they have to use it to make a sentence about two objects in the classroom. For example, *The board is higher than the rubbish bin.* If the sentence is correct, they stay where they are; if not, they move back to where they started. They cannot use an example that another player has already used.
- The winner is the first child to reach Finish.

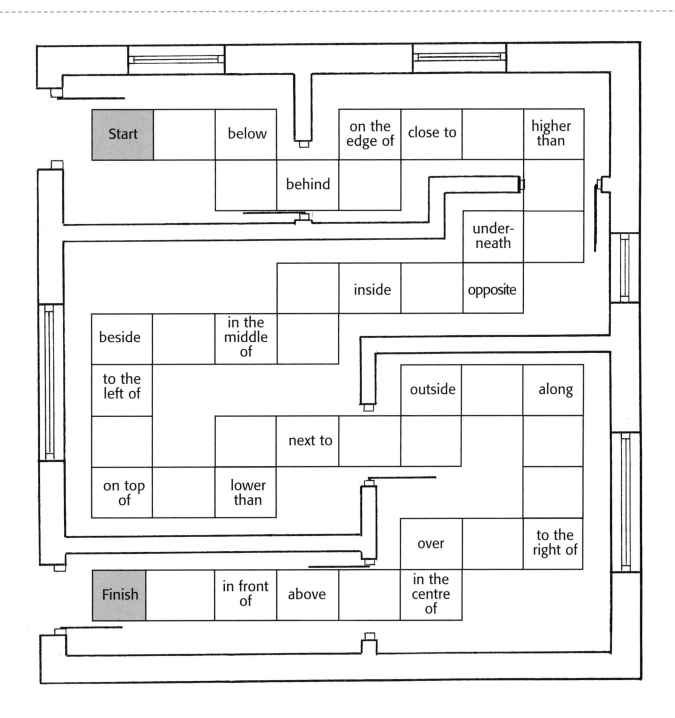

15.3 ▷ Treasure maps

 2

What you need

- squared paper and pencil per child

What to do

- Each child marks a 10 × 10 square on their piece of paper. Child A then secretly marks where their treasure is buried. Starting from the bottom left square, they describe the route to the square containing the treasure. The Child B draws the route as it is described. When they arrive at the treasure, they compare their grids to see if they have reached the correct square.
- Children reverse roles and repeat the activity.

15.4 ▷ Find the bear

 group/ whole class

What you need

- two different soft toys

What to do

- Split the class or group into two teams and blindfold one child from each team. Assign one soft toy to each team and hide the two toys in different places. Position the blindfolded children at roughly the same distance from their respective toys, preferably with some obstacles, such as a table or a bookcase, in between.
- Explain to the teams that they have to guide their blindfolded player to the toy, but they can only use the following words: left, right, up, down, turn, clockwise, anticlockwise, forward, stop, step(s), one, two, three, and so on. Write these on the board if necessary.
- Turn the blindfolded children around two or three times and start both teams at the same time. The first to find their toy is the winner.

Variation

After the child has found the toy, their team has to guide them back to the starting point.

15.5 ▷ Simon says turn

 group/ whole class

What you need

- no resources needed

What to do

- One child is chosen as the caller. The other children stand facing the caller who gives instructions such as *Simon says turn clockwise*. If the instruction is prefixed with *Simon says*, the children should carry out the instruction. If not, they should stand still. If appropriate, encourage children to specify whole, half or quarter turns.
- If children move in the wrong direction or at the wrong time, they lose a life. When a child loses three lives, they are out.
- The winner is the last child left in. They can be the caller next time the game is played.